A CARTOON GUIDE TO HOLINESS BY *Mike*

Redemptorist Publications

ISBN 0 85231 071 4

First printing November 1983
Second printing September 1984

Printed by Portia Press, Whitchurch, Hants

Saints...

. . . are in tune with
themselves

. . . are good listeners

Saints...

. . . are adventurous

. . . are wide awake!

. . . *are considerate*

. . . *are fun to be with*

Saints...

... have lots of heart

... share

... *think positively*   ... *keep on going on*

Saints...

... don't wear masks

... put other people first

. . . turn the other cheek

. . . sometimes fail

Saints...

. . . see the good in everyone

. . . don't know all
the answers

. . . sometimes look foolish

. . . find God in their hearts

Saints...

. . . aren't afraid to take a good look at themselves

. . . like to be in harmony

. . . don't hide away

. . . know when to take a rest

Saints...

... take one step
at a time

... know that everybody
is somebody

. . . respect other opinions

. . . usually travel incognito

Saints...

. . . use time wisely

. . . spread a little happiness

. . . blow away gloom

*. . . don't brood
on past failures*

Saints...

. . . think kind thoughts

. . . don't take themselves
too seriously

. . . need other people

. . . never stop learning

Saints...

. . . come in all sizes

. . . bear one another's burdens

. . . know they need forgiveness

. . . often look remarkably like mothers

Saints...

... know smiles are returned

... keep on growing

. . . *don't cling*

. . . *accept themselves
as they are*

Saints...

. . . speak no evil

. . . travel light

. . . don't talk too much

. . . live in love

Saints...

. . . *know when to be solemn*

. . . *know when to celebrate*

. . . know they are loved

. . . know when to bend a little

Saints...

... *have their ups and downs*

... *laugh at themselves*

. . . keep it simple

. . . flow with the universe

Saints...

. . . come in all shades

. . . often say
"Thank You"

. . . understand

. . . don't shout about it

Saints...

. . . enjoy a good laugh

. . . inhabit a friendly world

*. . . don't despise
simple pleasures*

. . . fit in nicely

Saints...

. . . often stand and stare

. . . co-operate

. . . always find
<u>another</u> way

. . . know they are beloved

Saints...

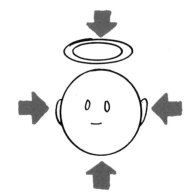

. . . start from where they are

. . . find wealth
in contentment

*. . . don't lock
themselves in*

. . . know how to sit quietly

Saints...

. . . flower in due season

. . . sing inside

. . . love holidays

. . . know flowers grow
even while they sleep

Saints...

... can take a few knocks

... pop up
in unexpected places

. . . glow

. . . accept

Saints...

. . . keep open hearts

. . . do little things well

. . . are seekers

. . . wait expectantly

Saints...

. . . rise after a fall

. . . live in the present

... know they are
vulnerable

... are children at heart

Saints...

. . . are loyal

. . . are gracious receivers

. . . are sympathetic

. . . are often made in pairs